On the Farm

By Julie Ferris

CELEBRATION PRESS
Pearson Learning Group

Contents

Farmers at Work 3

Sheep Shearing 4

Milking the Cows 10

Planting and Harvesting 16

Farms Around the World 20

Glossary 23

Index 24

Farmers at Work

All over the world, farmers are hard at work. Some farmers grow and **harvest** grain, vegetables, fruit, and flower **crops**. Other farmers raise animals such as sheep, goats, and cows for wool, meat, and milk. Farmers in different **regions** of the world often produce different things.

Meet three farmers with very different farms. Don Josè raises sheep, Mary runs a **dairy** farm, and Ben grows vegetables. Find out what happens on a busy day on their farms.

Don Josè Rajcevic is a sheep farmer in Chile.

Mary Mead is a dairy farmer in the United Kingdom.

Ben Burkett is a vegetable farmer in the United States.

Sheep Shearing

Sheep farmer Don Josè Rajcevic's *estancia* (es-tan-SEE-a), or ranch, is in southern Chile. It is in a rugged region, that has a cold **climate**. The *estancia* is very large. It covers 27 square miles and has both mountains and flat, grassy areas.

Don Josè raises 3,600 sheep. The sheep grow a woolly **fleece** that keeps them warm. Don Josè sells the woolly fleece. Wool is an important **product** for the ranch.

SOUTH AMERICA

N

Chile

Don Josè's *estancia*

Don José raises thousands of sheep.

Every day Don Josè and his farmworkers ride around the *estancia* on horseback to check on the sheep. The sheep **graze** on grassland. Sometimes wild animals called pumas come

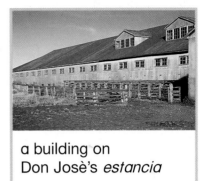

a building on Don Josè's *estancia*

down from the mountains and attack the sheep. The workers take dogs with them to scare the pumas away.

Don Josè and his workers ride horses around the *estancia*.

The sheep are herded into the shearing shed.

January 2003

One day in January the weather was warm, and it was time to **shear** the sheep. The farmworkers used dogs to help them **herd** the sheep. The sheep were rounded up into the *galpón* (gal-POHN), or shearing shed. Inside the *galpón*, the sheep were split up into groups. Each group waited in a separate shearing stall.

The sheep were sheared inside the stalls.
The shearers held the sheep in place with their feet.
Then the shearers leaned over the sheep to clip
the wool. They used electric shears with long cords
in order to reach all parts of the sheep.

"It takes just one minute to shear one sheep
and six days to shear all the sheep on the *estancia*,"
explained Don Josè.

The shearers are very skilled and are careful not to hurt
the sheep. They shear with long, smooth strokes.
This way the fleece rolls off in one piece.

The sheep are held in their stall until the whole group
has been sheared.

After shearing, the sheep were herded back
to the grassland. The wool was collected from the
floor and taken to the selecting tables. The best
wool was sorted and taken away to be packed.

At the selecting table
wool sorters check
each fleece for
length and quality.

The best wool is packed up in wool bales and is ready to be shipped.

The wool from Don Josè's *estancia* is shipped to the United Kingdom, where it is used to make clothes. Because January is one of the warmest months of the year in Chile, the sheep don't miss their woolly coats. Each year they grow a new fleece in time for the winter.

Wool Products

| spun yarn | knitted sweater | woolly hat | blankets |

When the wool arrives in the United Kingdom, it is washed, dried, and dyed different colors. People can make fabric and clothes from the wool.

Milking the Cows

Mary Mead is a dairy farmer. She owns a farm in Somerset, England, in the United Kingdom. Every day Mary feeds her cows wheat and grass, and every day they give milk in return.

Mary raises Friesian cows on the farm.

N

United Kingdom

England

Mary's farm

England has a mild climate with plenty of rain. It is ideal for growing food for the cows. The grass grows well during the spring, summer, and fall months. During these months Mary's cows go out to the fields to graze. In the winter the cows eat hay and grain that has been stored for the cooler months.

In the winter the cows stay in a warm barn. They eat food that has been stored.

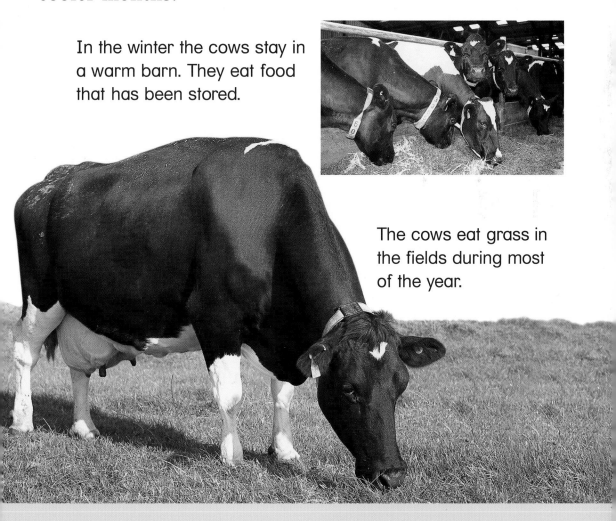

The cows eat grass in the fields during most of the year.

In the milking barn the cows are connected to milking machines.

September 2002

Mary's 400 cows are milked twice a day. One day in September the first milking began at five o'clock in the morning. Workers took the cows to the milking barn. The barn has a place for every cow to stand during the milking.

Next to each place is a long hose with small cups. First a farmhand cleaned the cows' udders. Udders are the sacs on a cow's underside that store milk. Then the farmworker put a cup on each teat, the place where the milk comes out of a cow.

The milk flowed from the cows. It went through the hoses to big tanks. The tanks collected the milk from all the cows. About twenty cows were milked at the time.

A farm worker cleans the cows' udders.

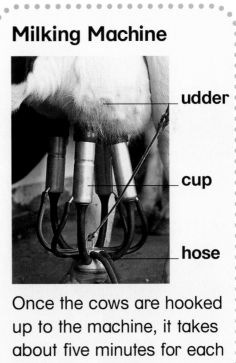

Milking Machine

udder

cup

hose

Once the cows are hooked up to the machine, it takes about five minutes for each cow to be milked.

After the milking the cows went back to the field. They ate grass and rested. At four o'clock in the afternoon, Mary led the cows back to the milking barn. They didn't need much help. They knew where to go and what to do.

During milking the farmworkers checked that the cows were healthy. "A good farmer will know all of the cows individually," explained Mary. "She can say hello to the cows and establish a relationship with them."

Mary and her farm manager
check the computer.
She records information
about the cows.

After the second milking the cows went back
to the field for the night. A truck picked up the milk
and delivered it to a dairy. Mary headed to her
office to do some other work. Mary and her cows
had finished the milking for one day.

Milk Products

butter   cheese   yogurt   ice cream

Milk can be used to make many different foods.

Planting and Harvesting

Ben Burkett has been a farmer for thirty years. He grows vegetables and **timber** on his 250-acre farm in Mississippi, in the southern part of the United States. "My family has farmed this land for 120 years," said Ben.

Mississippi has a warm climate. This means Ben can grow vegetables and fruit year-round. In the winter he grows leafy greens such as spinach and mustard greens. In the summer he grows peppers, sweet corn, eggplant, cucumbers, and watermelon.

In the winter months Ben grows turnips.

United States

Mississippi

Ben's Farm

N

April 2003

In April winter crops were ready to harvest and sell. Ben's family helped out with the harvesting. They picked the vegetables by hand. However, the winter of 2002–2003 was colder than usual, and some of Ben's crops died. That meant there were fewer crops than usual to harvest.

Ben and his farmworkers then prepared to plant summer vegetables. First, they had to **plow** the fields. Ben used a plow to turn the soil. Then he used another machine to break down chunks of soil and make the ground smoother.

Finally, Ben and his team planted the seeds using very large tractors. Ben planted crops that would be ready to harvest later in the summer. The crops take between seventy and one hundred days to grow.

Sweet corn takes eighty days to grow.

Ben checks his spring sweet corn crop.

On most days Ben and his workers finish working in the fields at six o'clock in the evening, but Ben's long day isn't over then. He travels to the nearby farmers' **co-operative**. At the co-operative, local farmers work together to wash and package their crops and get them ready for sale to grocery stores.

Vegetables from Ben's farm are packed into trucks. They are shipped to stores all over the eastern part of the United States. Ben's crops are sent to market as he ends his day on the farm.

At the co-operative, Ben packs boxes of vegetables into trucks.

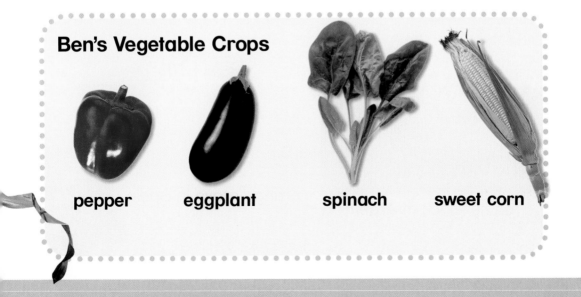

Ben's Vegetable Crops

pepper   eggplant   spinach   sweet corn

Farms Around the World

Most regions of the world produce farm products. Oranges grow well in Spain's warm climate. Australia has some of the largest sheep farms in the world. Farmers often choose to farm products based on the climate and land where they live.

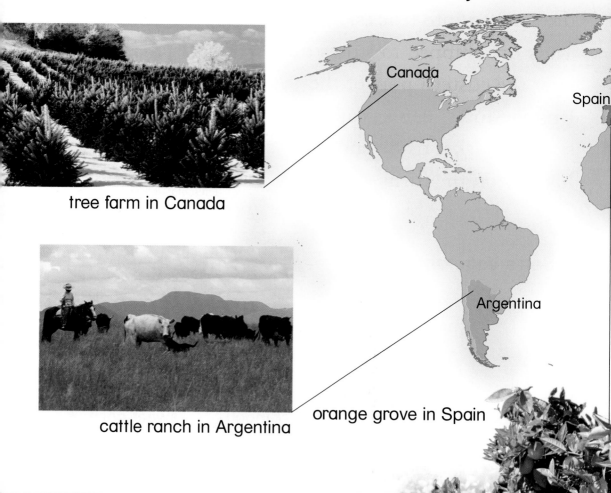

tree farm in Canada

cattle ranch in Argentina

orange grove in Spain

Canada

Spain

Argentina

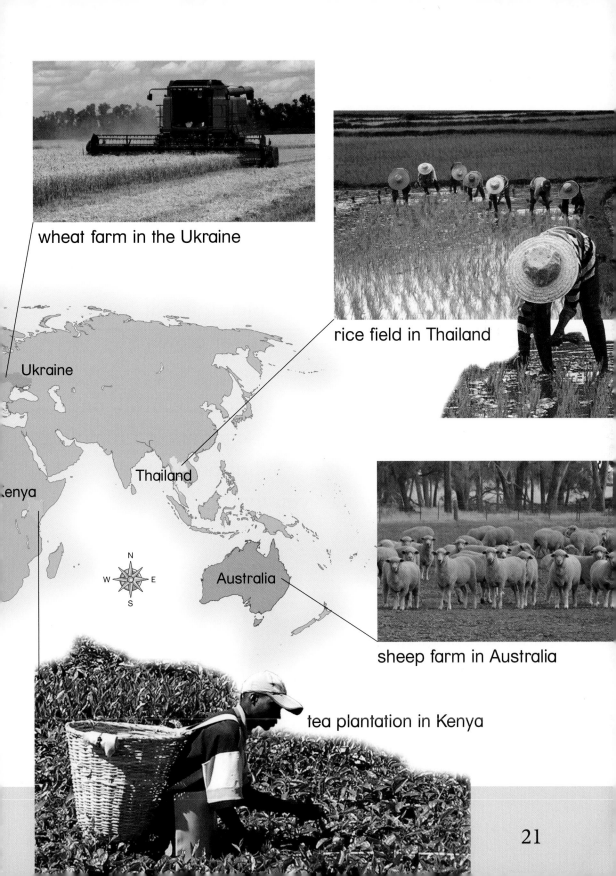

wheat farm in the Ukraine

rice field in Thailand

Ukraine

Kenya

Thailand

Australia

sheep farm in Australia

tea plantation in Kenya

21

Ben's crops would not grow on Don Josè's ranch in Chile because of the cold climate. However, Ben can harvest his crops year-round in the warm Mississippi climate. Don Josè's flock of sheep do well on the rugged grassland. Likewise Mary's cows have plenty to eat because the climate in England is ideal for growing their food.

Each region has its own climate, rainfall, and soil. So, farmers usually choose plants or animals that do well in their area. What products do farmers produce where you live?

Glossary

climate the kind of weather a place has from year to year

co-operative an organization that is owned and run by the people who work in it

crops plants that people grow and use

dairy relating to a place that produces milk or milk products

fleece a coat of wool on a sheep

graze to feed on grass or other plants

harvest to collect grown plants

herd to gather or keep together in a group

plow to turn up soil

product something that is made or grown

regions land areas that have special features

shear to cut the fleece off an animal

timber wood gained from trees

Index

Argentina 20

Australia 20, 21

Burkett, Ben 3,
    16–19, 22

Canada 20

Chile 3, 4, 22

co-operative 19

cows 3, 10–15, 20, 22

England 10, 11, 22

estancia 4, 5, 7, 9

farmer 3, 19, 20
    dairy 3, 10–15
    sheep 3, 4–9, 21, 22
    vegetable 3,
    16–19

fruit 3, 16, 20

Kenya 21

Mead, Mary 3, 10–12,
    14–15, 22

milking 10–15

milking machine 13

milk products 15

Mississippi 16, 22

planting 16–18

Rajcevic, Don Josè 3,
    4–5, 7–9, 22

shearing 6–8

sheep 3, 4–9, 20, 21, 22

Somerset 10

Spain 20

Thailand 21

Ukraine 21

United Kingdom 3, 9, 10

United States 3, 16

vegetables 3, 16–19

wool 3, 4, 9